T0128582

Gabby's A B C's

Jill Aubin

To order additional copies of this book, contact:
Xlibris
1-888-795-4274
www.Xlibris.com
Orders@Xlibris.com

Illustrated by Sierra Mon Ann Vidal

ISBN: 978-1-7960-5452-1 (sc)
ISBN: 978-1-7960-5451-4 (e)

Library of Congress Control Number: 2019912427

Print information available on the last page

Rev. date: 03/09/2021

This Book is
Dedicated to:
My Mom, My
Dad, Gabby and
My husband.

Inspired by: A Very Special Girl

A is for Angel.

  B is for Bubbles.

C is for Cuddles.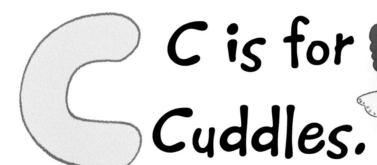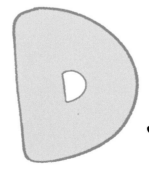

 D is for Dreams.

E is for
everyone.

F is for
flowers.

G is for
God.

H is for Heaven.

I is for, I love you.

J is for joy.

K is for kindness.

L is for Love.

M is for mom.

N is for nice.

O is for one, the one that I love.

P is for Princess.

Q is for quiet time.

R is for rainbow.

S is for smile.

T is for trust.

U is for Uplifting.

V is for violets.

W is for winner.

X is for
XOXO
(Hugs and Kisses)

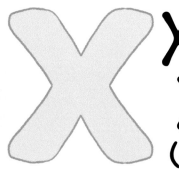

Y is for
You and
all that
you do.

zzZzᶻ

Z is
for zzz

Now it is
time to go
to sleep.

Printed in the United States
by Baker & Taylor Publisher Services